THE LAWS
OF
ANGLING

A Stringer Full of
Fishing's Eternal Verities

THE LAWS
OF
ANGLING

A Stringer Full of
Fishing's Eternal Verities

Randy Voorhees

**Andrews McMeel
Publishing**

Kansas City

For my grandmothers, Evelyn and Ruth,
who taught me the value of learning.

www.andrewsmcmeel.com

99 00 01 02 03 RDH 10 9 8 7 6 5 4 3 2

ISBN: 0-8362-7876-3

Library of Congress Catalog Card Number: 98-87736

Design by Holly Camerlinck

Introduction

I have been fishing—nobody calls it *angling* except for book publishers who want their offerings to sound more exalted—for all but four of my forty years. Most of the time I'm pretty good at it. However, I must admit that there have been occasions when things didn't go as planned.

There was the time I lost my balance while attempting to unsnag a hook from some branches and somersaulted head over heels—witnesses say I did a full 360-degree flip—into the Delaware Raritan Canal. Fortunately, I was unhurt and all my equipment was saved.

Another time I arrived streamside on the Raritan River at first daylight, anxious to get a jump on the competition. I had just purchased a new rod-and-reel combo the previous evening for a cool $120. I was standing on a rock, my freezing digits struggling to tie on a hook, when the line slipped through my hands and the rod and reel, all $120 worth, found its way to the bottom of the swollen river. Mildly agitated, I stripped down to my underwear and probed the riverbed with my toes, but to no avail. I was back at home before the rooster even warmed up.

I have taken turns with fishing buddies embedding hooks into one another's flesh. I once hooked my Labrador retriever with a spinning lure (he recovered quickly). I've fallen from docks, boats, banks, and from shallow water into deeper. I've arrived streamside with no line on my reel, and, of course, I've forgotten to bring my fishing license along on the same day that the game warden asked to see it. I didn't understand how these things could happen to me, a man who has fished for decades. Then it hit me!

The sport has a set of rules that govern all who fish: the laws of angling. In a more generic context, these *laws* are often associated with a certain Mr. Murphy. Murphy was undoubtedly an angler (probably one of those fancy-Dan fly-fishing boys all decked out in tweed). The *laws* prove that there are forces at work in angling that enforce a tenuous balance between man and fish.

The fish often pays with his life for taking our hook. It's only reasonable that the laws of angling exist to level the playing field. The *laws* will warn you of the trials and travails that await you, rod in hand, line in water, body in boat. They will give you cause to ponder: How can I lose to a fish?

Read on and find out.

 4

Fish in the water are
always larger than fish
out of the water.

The fishing was always better yesterday.

 6

The average tackle box
needs its own trailer
but never contains
the right lure.

Your boat motor
won't stop working
until you reach
the center of the lake.

8

The more expensive
your equipment,
the less fish
you will catch.

A thunderstorm spotted on Doppler radar at a distance of five hundred miles will reach the lake in the same time it takes you to turn off the TV and drive two miles.

Only when the storm
reaches the lake,
in a position
directly over your
head, will it stall.

11

Anyone
who refers to himself
as an "angler"
can't catch fish.

12

"Catch and release"
fishing has lifted
the burden of proof
from forty million
fishermen.

The surest way
to catch a big fish
is to buy a small net.

Fish don't ingest
lead sinkers voluntarily.

No one can outfish
a beginner.

If there is one tree
within three miles
of your boat
your lure will become
tangled in it.

It's as easy to catch a record-size fish as it is to get your spouse to rise at four A.M. to make your breakfast.

No one has yet found
a more effective
lure or bait
than dynamite.

Your boat won't sink
until you take
your boss fishing.

19

You can't learn anything from fishing books and videos. But you have to buy a lot of them to find that out.

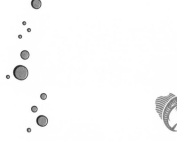

You won't get a "backlash" until the first cast of the day.

Nobody's exactly sure when the first fish story was told. Probably what happened was about a million years ago a couple of cavemen were standing near a stream with sticks, string, and worms in their hands when they noticed a trout swim past.

One caveman said, "Hey, let's try and catch that trout." And the other said, "Nah, let's just tell everyone we did."

Your odds of landing a world-record fish are absolutely zero unless:

1. You are fishing alone, in which case they are one in one million.

2. You are fishing alone, and you called in sick in order to go

fishing, in which case they
are one in one thousand.

3. You are fishing with your
girlfriend, and you told your wife
you were going on a business
retreat in the desert, in which
case you are even money to
smash the world record.

If you must quit in five minutes, the fish will start biting.

Waders leak only when you're more than a mile from the car.

A storm never
blows in
when the action is slow.

If you need to cast
farther to reach fish, the
wind will be in your
face.

Wearing tweed is the same as wearing a sign that says I HAVE MORE MONEY THAN SKILL.

No matter how bad the
fishing is, lightning will
make it worse.

A wake caused by a passing boat will not reach you until the exact millisecond you stand to cast.

The less skilled the fisherman, the more likely he is to share his thoughts about equipment, technique, and promising hot spots.

The less affluent the fisherman, the more likely he is to have the most expensive equipment.

It's morally wrong
to cast across another
angler's line,
unless, of course,
he's outfishing you.

Fly-fishing is easy to
learn, like calculus
or the golf swing.

The worst anglers
are the earliest risers.

The definition of "angler" is a person who is passionate about matching wits with a fish.

Anglers who don't lie
about the size
of their catch
are as common
as free lunches.

Forget the bait
but not
the mosquito repellent.

In the absence of a life preserver, your fishing companions make excellent flotation devices.

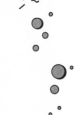

Honesty is as
important in fishing
as it is in golf.

If your companion
hasn't fished the lake
or river before,
don't be a spoilsport
and ruin
all the surprises.

The surest way
to get skunked is to
pack a camera.

When you ask an angler "Had any luck?," you should regard his response as his opening offer.

Never bet on catching the biggest fish until after you've sabotaged your competitor's equipment.

 44

Trust a friend with
your life if you must,
but never divulge
the location of
your best fishing hole.

The first thing
you catch after
sharpening your hooks
will be your ear.

A pool of rising trout
means you forgot
your fly rod.

If you catch a fish,
the odds against
catching two double.

A wonderful intellect is
as essential to
an angler as a
conscience is to
a lawyer.

There are lies, damn lies, and fish stories. The difference is that the first two are offered with the hope that someone might believe.

Never fish with
anyone who offers you
a helmet.

For anglers, NO
FISHING translates to
"Hey, come on in guys.
This means everyone
but you."

51

A bad day fishing
is just that:
a bad day.

You can hit a
ten-acre lake with your
lure about half the time,
and a branch one inch
in diameter every time.

Each time an angler catches a fish he must lose twenty-five dollars worth of equipment to restore the normal balance of fishing economics.

The bamboo used to
make expensive
fishing rods is the same
material used
in Singapore
for caning people.

The divorce rate is
highest among couples
who fish together.

Fishing demands
patience *and* beer.

Parents who take their
children fishing get
what they deserve.

Few anglers are born
with a natural talent
for catching fish, but
nearly all could lie
like hell while they
were still in diapers.

 58

For most anglers,
the only difference
between expensive
equipment and
cheap equipment
is the price.

There is no creel limit
on jet skiers.

Real men
don't buy bait
from vending machines.

There aren't any
hyphenated names
among catfishermen.

If your favorite lake is empty when you arrive, it's because the horn is about to sound, signaling the start of a thousand-boat fishing tournament.

The best way to find
a lost rod and reel
is to buy replacements.

For every bass
fisherman named Pierre
there are one hundred
named Billy Ray
or Jethro.

People who buy
expensive homes
on fishing lakes always
hate fishermen.

If you plan on keeping
the fish you catch, you'll
need a place to bury them
after you realize
you have no idea how to
clean or cook them.

The best weather
for fishing will be
on any day
you can't go.

Anglers maintain
a ratio of three
wall-mounted fish
to every one
family portrait.

Large legendary fish are always given a name—usually Bubba—out of respect for their ability to outsmart an angler.

On the seventh day God made TNN (The Nashville Network).

First-aid kits are for pessimists and sissies.

If you fall into the water it's perfectly all right to save your life *before* checking to see if anyone saw you fall.

Always ask
before dipping
your spoon into
any container
in a fisherman's
refrigerator.

Never believe
anything you hear on
The Weather Channel.

An angler's ability to catch fish is in inverse proportion to the number of flies he has dangling from his hat.

Anglers are living proof
that fish is not
great brain food.

The surest way
to lose an expensive
fishing lure
is to use it.

Falling out of a boat
is a lot easier than
climbing into one.

Nobody ever lost
a little one.

If your plan is to eat your catch, pack a lunch.

Nobody asks to see your stringer unless they already know it's empty.

You can always find
your fishing license
in the same location
as your missing sock.

The four words
every angler most
hates to hear:
"I've got another one."

Anglers root for
each other
the way lawyers do.

Don't ever
weigh yourself
on an angler's scale.

 82

The only purpose
served by an electronic
fish finder is to show
exactly how many fish
are ignoring your bait.

Standing behind a fisherman is as perilous as peering over the shoulder of a man looking into his wallet.

More trophy fish
are bred in saloons
than are grown in all
the rivers and lakes.

Fish jump mostly
when amused.

Never travel across
state lines to fish when
you can get skunked
right at home.

The fundamental inequality of angling is that the fish pays with his life for his first mistake. There would be few anglers left if the tables were turned.

There is no greater joy
than watching a
companion lose a big fish.

The quickest way to meet
a game warden is to
forget your license.

Your first attempt to navigate a strange boat ramp will be witnessed by exactly four million snickering know-it-alls and one spouse who wants to know "what they're all laughing at."

A real fisherman has
the local bait shop on
speed dial.

90

Never fish a stream
inhabited by
hungry bears
unless accompanied by
a slow-footed friend.

Calling in sick
to go fishin' is as true
a form of Americana
as moms and apple pie.